D0458286

Why I Live in
VIRGINIA

101 Dang Good Reasons

Ellen Patrick

ISBN 1-58173-399-2

Jacket and text design by Miles G. Parsons
Printed in Italy

1. Can you say "founding fathers"?

2. Not to be too snobby about it, but we invented America.

3. What do you mean the South will rise again? When were we not on top?

4. More U.S. presidents per square mile.

—∿—

5. If there is a horse race, we're in it.

6. If there is a horse race, we're winning it.

—〜〜—

7. State troopers are good at keeping tourists in line.

8. Black bears are good at keeping tourists in line.

9. If you get tired of the Tidewater, there's always the Piedmont.

10. If you get tired of the Piedmont, there's always the Blue Ridge.

11. If you get tired of the Blue Ridge, there's always the Appalachians.

12. Only state called home by both Southerners and Yankees.

13. Better than living in West Virginia.

—⁓—

14. The Hokies kick Atlantic Conference butt.

15. More Confederate generals per square mile.

16. More NASCAR tracks per square mile.

17. Ham so good you'll slap your mama. And her mama.

18. Boiled peanuts.

—⁓—

19. Sweet tea.

20. The Blue Ridge in spring.

—⁓—

21. The fiddling convention in Galax.

22. Ever heard of country music? We invented it.

23. Other states think we're snobs, but they're just jealous.

24. First Manassas.

—⚬—

25. Second Manassas.

26. We know what a cooter is. Do you?

—⁓—

27. Winchester at apple blossom time.

28. The Blue Ridge in fall.

—◊◊—

29. The U.S. Navy seems to think this is a good place to call home.

30. If you ain't been to Virginia Beach, you ain't partied.

31. There's only one place that might be prettier. It's called paradise.

32. Go U.V. Cavaliers!

—◆—

33. Children who still say "please" and "thank you."

34. Neighbors so friendly you might risk an overdose of pound cake.

35. The Blue Ridge in summer.

—⚬—

36. It's fun giving Yankee tourists directions.

37. Scenic islands with wild horses? No problem.

38. Exact replicas of colonial villages? No problem.

39. Impeccably preserved presidential mansions?
No problem.

40. Misty mountains and endless vistas? No problem.

—⁓—

41. Re-enactors remind the rest of us we are sane.

42. Fishing so good it induces delirium.

---⁓⁓⁓---

43. Antique junkies who will never kick the habit.

44. Last bastion of good manners.

—ᴖᴖ—

45. Last bastion of the Blue Plate Special.

46. We learn to play stringed instruments, then we learn to walk.

47. We commute to D.C., and thank heavens, we commute home again.

48. Excuse us, but are YOU a commonwealth? We didn't think so.

49. Old Dominion. Translation: older, bigger, better.

50. Sic semper tyrannis.

—⟋⟋⟋—

51. Dogwoods in spring.

52. Stonewall Jackson's horse buried here.

———— ⸕⸕⸕ ————

53. Stonewall Jackson's arm buried here.

54. The rest of Stonewall Jackson buried here.

—〰—

55. Lynchburg: world leader in concrete lawn ornaments.

56. No shortage of churches.

—◆—

57. Families who still eat dinner together.

58. Families who still cook their dinner.

—⁂—

59. Families who still cook their breakfast and lunch.

60. Children who still say "sir" and "ma'am."

—◦◦◦—

61. If it was good enough for John Boy Walton, it's good enough for me.

62. Fast cars.

—⚬⚬⚬—

63. Fast horses.

—⚬⚬⚬—

64. Slow talkin'.

65. Hushpuppies.

—〰—

66. If it's a team sport, we play it.

67. People who don't live here console themselves by singing songs about us.

68. People who don't live here console themselves by making movies about us.

69. People who don't live here console themselves by reading books about us.

70. We don't really need a reason to live here. We're Virginians.

71. West Virginia is almost heaven. This IS heaven.

—〰—

72. Virginia is for lovers—and everyone else.

73. Underground caverns where you can imagine all sorts of crazy things.

74. So many lighthouses we border on being too picturesque.

75. We welcome transplants and consider them natives immediately—after 40 or 50 years.

76. It's fun to talk as slow as possible and watch Yankees cross their eyes.

—⁓—

77. Johnny Appleseed slept here.

78. If you get enough of this life, you can visit the afterlife at the Edgar Cayce Institute.

79. Where else are you going to see the world's largest cured ham?

80. Where else are you going to see the world's oldest peanut museum?

81. Liz Taylor could have married a senator from anywhere, but she picked here.

82. There may be some other place in the universe with better apples, but it's unlikely.

83. There may be some other place in the universe with nicer people, but it's unlikely.

84. There may be some other place in the universe with prettier mountains, but it's unlikely.

85. Hiking so good you might never stop.

—⁂—

86. Camping so good you might never stop.

87. Canoeing so good you might never stop.

—⁂—

88. Sightseeing so good you might never stop.

89. Ooh, those tourist dollars sure spend good.

90. Can you say "homemade biscuits"?

—◈—

91. When it snows, we get to have a great big party.

92. If it was good enough for George Washington, it's good enough for me.

93. There's no place like home—if you live in Virginia.

—◊—

94. Only state named after a virgin queen. (Don't laugh!)

95. Captain Smith and Pocahontas had the right idea.

—∞—

96. Sunsets over the Shenandoah Valley.

97. Inns that presidents once slept in.

—∞—

98. Cardinals in the dogwoods.

99. Steeplechase races.

—⁂—

100. More Civil War history per square mile.

101. You can leave Virginia, but you'll always come home again.